D1589502

Other titles from IES:

New Directions in Management Development
Hirsh W, Carter A
IES Report 387, 2002. ISBN 1 85184 316 7

Work-Life Balance: Beyond the Rhetoric
Kodz J, Harper H, Dench S
IES Report 384, 2002. ISBN 1 85184 313 2

Partnership Under Pressure: How Does it Survive?
Reilly P
IES Report 383, 2002. ISBN 1 85184 312 4

Costing Sickness Absence in the UK
Bevan S, Hayday S
IES Report 382, 2001. ISBN 1 85184 311 6

Executive Coaching: Inspiring Performance at Work
Carter A
IES Report 379, 2001. ISBN 1 85184 308 6

The Problem of Minority Performance in Organisations
Tackey ND, Tamkin P, Sheppard E
IES Report 375, 2001. ISBN 1 85184 304 3

A Share of the Spoils: employee financial participation
Reilly P, Cummings J, Bevan S
IES Report 373, 2001. ISBN 1 85184 303 5

Succession Planning Demystified
Hirsh W
IES Report 372, 2000. ISBN 1 85184 302 7

Free, Fair and Efficient? Open internal job advertising
Hirsh W, Pollard E, Tamkin P
IES Report 371, 2000. ISBN 1 85184 301 9

A catalogue of these and over 100 other titles is available from IES, or on the IES Website, www.employment-studies.co.uk

the Institute
for Employment
Studies

Kirkpatrick and Beyond:

a review of training evaluation

P Tamkin
J Yarnall
M Kerrin

IES Research Networks

I E S

Report 392

Published by:

THE INSTITUTE FOR EMPLOYMENT STUDIES
Mantell Building
Falmer
Brighton BN1 9RF
UK

Tel.   + 44 (0) 1273 686751
Fax   + 44 (0) 1273 690430

http://www.employment-studies.co.uk

British Cataloguing-in-Publication Data

A catalogue record for this publication is available from the British Library

ISBN 1 85184 321 3

Printed in Great Britain

The Institute for Employment Studies

IES is an independent, international and apolitical centre of research and consultancy in human resource issues. It works closely with employers in the manufacturing, service and public sectors, government departments, agencies, professional and employee bodies, and foundations. For over 30 years the Institute has been a focus of knowledge and practical experience in employment and training policy, the operation of labour markets and human resource planning and development. IES is a not-for-profit organisation which has a multidisciplinary staff of over 50. IES expertise is available to all organisations through research, consultancy, publications and the Internet.

IES aims to help bring about sustainable improvements in employment policy and human resource management. IES achieves this by increasing the understanding and improving the practice of key decision makers in policy bodies and employing organisations.

The IES Research Networks

This report is the product of a study supported by the IES Research Networks, through which Members finance, and often participate in, applied research on employment issues. Full information on Membership is available from IES on request, or at www.employment-studies.co.uk/networks/

L 100 TAM

Contents

Executive Summary

Training evaluation is a bit like eating five portions of fruit and vegetables a day; everyone knows that they are supposed to do it, everyone says they are planning to do better in the future and few people admit to having got it right.

Despite IiP, despite high levels of future intention (Industrial Society, 2000), many organisations are not satisfied that their methods of evaluating training are rigorous or extensive enough to answer questions of value to the organisation. And this is all despite the fact that there is a model of training evaluation that has been popular for decades, *ie* Kirkpatrick's four level model of training evaluation, beginning with immediate participant reactions to a training experience and ending with organisational impact.

It may be that the discomfort with our activity is because our models are no longer up to the job and need a serious overhaul. If this is so, who are the main contenders? In this review, we look critically at the Kirkpatrick model and compare it to others. We explore what these models might imply about the process of learning and changing behaviour, and we also review some of the research evidence on training evaluation that throws light on issues associated with evaluating at different levels.

Kirkpatrick

Kirkpatrick developed his four-step model in 1959 and provided a simple and pragmatic model for helping practitioners think about training programmes. It has, however, been criticised for implying a hierarchy of value related to the different levels, with organisational performance measures being seen as more important that reactions. More fundamentally, there have been criticisms of the assumption that the levels are each associated with the previous and next levels. This implied causal relationship has not always been established by research. Other complaints are that the model is too simple and fails to take account of the various intervening variables affecting learning and transfer.

Descendant models

In response, others have developed models of their own that purport to resolve some of these difficulties. Several of these might be thought of as Kirkpatrick progeny, in that they take much that was inherent in the original model and extend it either at the front end, with the inclusion of training design or needs analysis, or back end, with an evaluation of societal outcomes — and sometimes both. We consider six models in detail and a further five more briefly.

Fresh blood

Other models are unrelated to Kirkpatrick, having a rather different approach to how training evaluation might take place. These include:

- responsive evaluation (Pulley, 1994), which focuses on what decision makers in the organisation would like to know and how this might be met
- context evaluation (Newby, 1992), which focused on appropriate evaluation for different contexts, and
- evaluative enquiry (Preskill and Torres, 1999), which approaches evaluation as a learning experience using dialogue, reflection and challenge to distil learning opportunities, to create a learning environment and to develop enquiry skills.

The final group of models emphasise the importance of different measures of impact, including the learning outcomes approach of Kraiger *et al.* (1993) linking training evaluation to cognitive, skill-based and affective learning outcomes, and the balanced scorecard approach of Kaplan and Norton (1996), which focuses on different perspectives of finance, customers and internal processes.

An underlying model

All of the models tacitly base themselves on an assumption that there is a chain of impact from a developmental process to individual learning, changed behaviour and resulting organisational or social impact. However, they rarely make such a model explicit, and therefore they are all open to the criticism that they ignore some of the key variables that impact on this chain of events. We explore what such a model of learning might include, that recognises the intervening factors affecting the strength of the relationship between one link in the chain and the next. Such a model is not necessarily a model of training evaluation with all the complexity inherent in a model of learning; rather it is meant to support the practitioner to undertake sensible and coherent evaluation of use to the organisation. Inevitably, this also involves knowing what not to evaluate, and simplification is a vital part of the evaluation process.

Evidence on issues affecting evaluation

Evaluating at different links in the chain (or at different Kirkpatrick levels) is affected by different variables. The evaluation ought at least to be cognisant of these, as they can affect the ability of one level to affect the level that follows it.

Reaction

At the reaction level, research has shown that there is relatively little correlation between learner reactions and measures of learning, or subsequent measures of changed behaviour (*eg* Warr *et al.*, 1999; Alliger and Janak, 1989; Holton, 1996). It has been suggested that 'satisfaction' is not necessarily related to good learning and sometimes discomfort is essential. Mixed results may indicate that what is measured at the reaction level stage might be important, and more focused reaction level questionnaires may be more informative about the value of training.

Learning

There is much literature encouraging the use of before-and-after questionnaires to gauge learning gain from courses. Some have urged caution, raising concerns that a trainee might be able to repeat what they have learnt but may not be able to apply it (Erikson, 1990), that performance during training may not be a predictor of post-training performance (Ghodsian *et al.*, 1997), that testing may not be appropriate for measuring the attainment of soft skills (Rough, 1994), or indeed for skills in general (Bee and Bee, 1994).

Behaviour change

There are a wealth of studies that comment on the failure of training to transfer into the workplace and which have identified a range of organisational factors that inhibit success. Warr *et al.* (1999) have identified the importance of organisational culture and learning confidence. The more difficult an individual found the training, the less likely they were to be able to apply it; the more supportive line managers were, the more likely the application of learning. Other important factors are perceived usefulness and job autonomy and commitment (Holton, 1996).

Similarly, there are a number of individual factors that influence transfer and application of learning; self-efficacy, motivation to learn, and general intelligence have all been associated (Salas and Cannon-Powers, 2001).

Not surprisingly, several have suggested that evaluation of behaviour change needs to become much more complex to take account of these factors. There have been suggestions of using manager- and self-assessment, but with concerns that they are not always accurate (Carless and Roberts-Thompson, 2001).

Organisational results

Whilst this is probably the most difficult level of evaluation, many writers have expounded the view that training must be evaluated using hard outcome data (*eg* Levin, 1983; Phillips, 1996; Kearns and Miller, 1997). The difficulties of doing so tend to be dismissed by these researchers. Others, however, express caution, pointing out the many assumptions that are made (Bee and Bee, 1994) or the inherent difficulties in linking soft skills training to hard results (Abernathy, 1999), the time delays that are rarely taken into account (Newby, 1992) and that hard measures miss much that is of value (Kaplan and Norton, 1996).

Organisational activity

The evidence from a range of research studies indicates that training evaluation has been steadily becoming more common (Deloitte, Haskins, Sells, 1989; Marginson *et al.*, 1993, Industrial Society, 2000), but that the predominant level of analysis is level 1, with very few attempting levels 3 or 4. Surprisingly, despite the emphasis on measuring business results, relatively few companies with comprehensive training evaluation, try to justify training spend (Blanchard *et al.*, 2000).

Our review would indicate that although there is an abundance of models that purport to improve on the Kirkpatrick model, there is a huge similarity in many of the models now on offer. The trends have been to extend the model to include the foundations for training and take into account the need that the training is meant to address. At the other end, the model extends to include measures of societal impact. The overall conclusion, however, is that the model remains very useful for framing where evaluation might be made. Organisations would do well to consider some of the findings of the issues that affect the linkage between the levels in the model. They need to think much more carefully about how they structure their reaction questionnaires, about the other factors that can inhibit the transfer of learning to the workplace, and what they might do to maximise impact.

The important message is: to conduct the best evaluation possible, that provides information that meets the needs of the organisation, within the inevitable constraints of organisational life.

1. Introduction

We place enormous faith in training and development. We hope it will raise national competitiveness (*eg* DTI, 2001), that it will improve UK management capability (*eg* Mabey and Thomson, 2000; Tamkin, Hillage and Willison, 2002), that it will confer competitive advantage and that it will improve individual employability. Like all faith, these beliefs exist and prosper regardless of supportive evidence. In fact evidence is hard to come by (Tamkin *et al.* 2002), tends to be difficult to gather, is patchy and incomplete. On the one hand we have growing pressure to improve and extend decent evaluation, whilst on the other hand there is some evidence that evaluation practice lags some way behind these exhortations (Industrial Society, 2000).

Part of this debate is on how organisations can evaluate training and development impact. Fully evaluating the impact of training is something of a holy grail for practitioners. Despite the push from Investors in People and the Kirkpatrick model of evaluation that has been in existence for decades, organisations still struggle to evaluate behaviour change and organisational impact effectively. The Kirkpatrick model has been much criticised, partly because of its age and a belief that the practice of evaluating development impact must have moved on over the last forty-odd years. Other models of training evaluation abound, all of which promise a more rigorous or more useful approach to evaluation. But do these alternative models really add anything new, is Kirkpatrick really past its sell-by date, or are we merely diverting our attention away from the real work of getting on with evaluation whilst we pontificate about how best to do it?

In this review, we provide a critical overview of the various models of training evaluation. Following a brief revisit to

Kirkpatrick's model, the review begins by outlining more recent evaluation models in the literature, some of which have modified or added to Kirkpatrick's framework, and some which have taken a different approach. The review then moves on to examine some of the issues involved in evaluation at each of Kirkpatrick's four levels, in order to provide some insights into the validity of the different models on offer. We also briefly review practice within organisations and finally comment on the evaluation process itself and what it is we are really attempting to do.

2. Evaluation Models

We begin by looking at the Kirkpatrick model and other models that are similar to it. We then go on to look at models that approach development evaluation from a different perspective, and what emerges from this comparison.

2.1 The four-level approach: Kirkpatrick (1959)

The best-known and most widely used framework for classifying evaluation is the Kirkpatrick model. The model consists of four stages, originally described as steps but described more recently by Kirkpatrick (1996) as levels (see Figure 2.1). The four levels are:

- **Level 1: Reaction** — what the participants thought of the programme, normally measured by the use of reaction questionnaires

- **Level 2: Learning** — the changes in knowledge, skills, or attitude with respect to the training objectives, normally assessed by use of performance tests

- **Level 3: Behaviour** — changes in job behaviour resulting from the programme, to identify whether the learning is being applied. Assessment methods include observation and productivity data.

- **Level 4: Results** — the bottom-line contribution of the training programme. Methods include measuring costs, quality and return on investment (ROI).

The strengths of Kirkpatrick's model lie in its simplicity and pragmatic way of helping practitioners think about training programmes (Alliger and Janak, 1989). It is easily comprehended

Figure 2.1: The Kirkpatrick four-level model

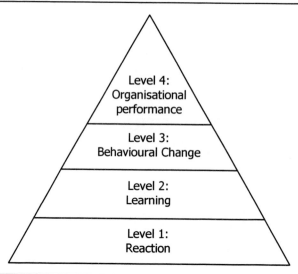

Source: from Kirkpatrick, 1996

and makes sense to organisations and has become the most commonly adopted model or framework on training evaluation. However, in recent years the four-level model has come under increasing criticism.

One of the common criticisms is based on a misunderstanding that the levels are arranged in ascending value of information, with results data being viewed as more important than reactions. Bernthal (1995) argues that the model mixes evaluation and effectiveness and that these do not form a continuum. However, the model was not meant to be seen as a hierarchy when it was first developed and it is clear that the value of the information will depend on the type of evaluation required. For example, it could be argued that levels 1 and 2 provide some of the most useful information, as these outcomes are often the easiest to measure and change (Bernthal, 1995).

There is also an assumption that each level is caused by or associated to the previous level. The implied causal relationship between each level has not been demonstrated by research (*eg* Lee and Pershing, 2000; Warr, Allan and Birdi, 1999). Indeed, many evaluation studies that have evaluated training on two or more of Kirkpatrick's levels have reported different effects of training for different levels (Alliger and Janak, 1989).

One of Kirkpatrick's main critics is Holton (1996). He argues that the levels form a taxonomy of outcomes rather than a model, due to the lack of constructs identified and the assumption of causal relationships that are not empirically tested. It is unlikely, however, that training managers will concern themselves with the distinction between a taxonomy and a model, and Kirkpatrick himself has stated that he doesn't care whether his four steps are considered a model or a taxonomy, providing training professionals find it useful in evaluating training programmes. However, Holton also states that no evaluation model can be validated without measuring and accounting for intervening variables that effect learning and transfer processes. Kraiger and Jung (in Quinones, 1997) agree with this view and argue that whilst Kirkpatrick provides a model for thinking about *how* to evaluate, it does little to inform *what* to evaluate and *how to link* the results to strategy. Like others, they criticise the model for its failure to incorporate recent psychological findings on learning and skill acquisition, as well as its ambiguity about how to operationalise measurement levels. This argument will be revisited later in this review.

2.2 Kirkpatrick plus

Research into the training evaluation models that have been proposed over the last 40 years since Kirkpatrick's framework, show that many have used the four levels as a basis for their thinking. This section aims to summarise the most frequently cited models to have used Kirkpatrick's framework as a starting point. It is not intended, at this stage, to debate the relative merits of each, but merely to draw out the differences, in order to assess the degree to which evaluation models have moved on.

2.2.1 The five-level approach: Hamblin (1974)

Hamblin was one of the first to modify Kirkpatrick's model. The first three levels in his model correspond closely to Kirkpatrick's model. However, the final level is split into two: organisation and ultimate value. The five level model is therefore:

- Level 1: Reactions
- Level 2: Learning
- Level 3: Job behaviour

- Level 4: Organisation — the effects on the organisation, from participant's job to performance changes

- Level 5: Ultimate Value — the financial effects, both on the organisation and the economy.

Unlike Kirkpatrick, Hamblin suggests that the five levels of his model form a hierarchy.

2.2.2 The Organisational Elements Model (OEM): Kaufman, Keller and Watkins (1995)

Kaufman and Keller (1994) argue that Kirkpatrick's model was intended for evaluating training, and that as organisations now seek to evaluate other types of development events, the framework needs to be modified. They expanded Kirkpatrick's model to include societal contribution as an evaluation criteria. They argue that manufacturing organisations in particular are increasingly being called to account for societal consequences such as pollution and safety.

The model also included some additions at the other levels, such as the inclusion of needs assessment and planning in the evaluation, an examination of the desired or expected results, and a review of the availability and quality of resources. They contend that evaluation at all levels should be planned and designed prior to the implementation of any intervention.

With the additional help of Watkins in 1995, the team re-classified the criterion in their model into the following six levels:

- Level 1: Input — similar to Kirkpatrick's reaction level, but has been expanded to include the role, usefulness, appropriateness and contributions of the methods and resources used.

- Level 2: Process — this level also has similarities to the reaction level, but is expanded to include an analysis of whether the intervention was implemented properly in terms of achieving its objectives.

- Level 3: Micro (acquisition) — this is similar to the learning level and examines individual as well as small-group mastery and competence.

- Level 4: Micro (performance) — links closely to the behaviour level and examines the utilisation of skills and knowledge. The focus is on application rather than transfer of skills and knowledge.

- Level 5: Macro — relates to the results level and examines organisational contributions and payoffs.
- Level 6: Mega — an additional level which looks at societal outcomes.

They argue that costs can be examined at each stage, from efficiency measures at the input level to utility costs at the highest level.

2.2.3 Indiana University approach: Molenda, Pershing and Reigheluth (1996)

Indiana University developed an evaluation taxonomy-based on six strata, which were not intended to be a hierarchy of importance. The first and last strata provide additions to Kirkpatrick's framework.

- Stratum 1: Activity accounting — which examines training volume and level per participant
- Stratum 2: Participant reactions
- Stratum 3: Participant learning
- Stratum 4: Transfer of training
- Stratum 5: Business impact
- Stratum 6: Social impact

The sixth stratum examines the impact of changed performance on society, and as such is similar to Hamblin's 'ultimate value' and Kaufman *et al.'s* 'societal impact'.

2.2.4 The Carousel of Development: Industrial Society (2000)

The Industrial society (now the Work Foundation) developed a six stage circular model which starts with a planning phase. The stages are:

- Stage 1: Identify the business need.
- Stage 2: Define the development objectives.
- Stage 3: Design the learning process.

- Stage 4: Experience the learning process.
- Stage 5: Use and reinforce the learning.
- Stage 6: Judge the benefits to the organisation (quality measures, customer satisfaction and financial benefits provide the main measures at this level).

The Industrial Society differentiated between stages 3 and 4, which aim to validate the training, and stages 5 and 6, which aim to evaluate it. Andrew Forrest at the Industrial Society argues that 'true evaluation needs to take place long before and after training has taken place' and that the process of identifying the business need is an essential component of the evaluation model.

2.2.5 The five-level ROI framework: Phillips (1994), Phillips and Holton (1995)

Phillips is known in the evaluation field for his focus on Return on Investment (ROI). His evaluation model is largely comparable to Kirkpatrick, but adds a fifth level to separate out the assessment of the monetary benefits of the training compared to its costs. The levels are:

- Reaction and planned action — which also includes a plan of what participants intend to apply from the programme
- Learning
- Job application
- Business results
- Return on Investment

Business results are assessed using measures such as quality, costs, time and customer satisfaction ratings.

2.2.6 The KPMT model: Kearns and Miller (1997)

Kearns and Miller's KPMT model has many similarities to Phillip's work. They argue that clear objectives are an essential component of a training evaluation model. Where Kearns and Miller differ is in their aim to provide a 'toolkit' to help evaluators work through the process of identifying bottom-line objectives through questioning techniques, evaluating existing training, and using process mapping to identify the added value to organisations.

They argue that training can only bring added value to organisations if the business is not performing effectively or there is a market opportunity which can be exploited. To identify bottom line benefits, pre-training measurements need to be in place. Only where the training is to bring someone up to the standards of the job is this not necessary.

The four-stage KPMT model starts at the beginning of the training cycle by identifying the business need rather than the training need. The emphasis is on clarifying objectives from a business perspective rather than that of the trainees. Despite this, the evaluation levels look very similar to Kirkpatrick's:

- Reaction to training and development
- Learning
- Transfer to the workplace/behaviour
- Bottom line added value, measured in relation to the base level measures taken.

The process they suggest to achieve this is:

- Step 1: Discuss the needs of the business.
- Step 2: Design some proposed training and development solutions.
- Step 3: Decide on the real training issues and get buy-in to these.
- Step 4: Deliver.
- Step 5: Evaluate.
- Step 6: Feed back the results.

Where Kearns and Miller differ from some of the other models is in their belief that return on investment can only be looked at in hard terms. They state that 'if a business objective cannot be cited as a basis for designing training and development, then no training and development should be offered'. As an example, they argue that if development aims to brings about greater awareness (*eg* of customers) then it should still only be measured by the eventual effect on hard measures such as customer spend and number of customers.

The per cent return on investment (ROI) is calculated as:

$$\frac{\text{benefits from training (\$)} - \text{costs of training (\$)}}{\text{costs of training (\$)}} \times 100$$

They dismiss the difficulties of attributing long-term financial gains directly to training, by arguing that it doesn't matter if other factors contribute. They suggest that by creating simple process flow maps, the causal connections can be made explicit.

2.2.7 CIRO (Context, Input, Reaction, Outcome) Approach: Warr, Bird and Rackham (1970)

The CIRO model suggests that prior to assessing reactions and outcomes there needs to be an analysis of the context and possible inputs. The four stages are:

- Context — the operational situation provides information that helps to determine the training needs and objectives.
- Input — information about possible training methods or techniques is gathered, to select the best choice of training intervention.
- Reaction — gathering participant views and suggestions about the training programme.
- Outcome — looking at the results of training at an immediate, intermediate and ultimate level.

The reaction level is similar to Kirkpatrick's, but with greater emphasis on suggestions to change the format of the training event. The outcome level straddles learning, behaviour and end results.

2.2.8 Bernthal (1995), Brinkerhoff (1987), Bushnell, (1990), Sleezer *et al.* (1992) and Fitz-enz (1994)

A few less well known models are also worth a mention. Bernthal (1995) suggests several additions to Kirkpatrick's model, including greater consideration of the context and development of a 'training-impact tree'. He suggests that the first steps in evaluation should be:

10   The Institute for Employment Studies

- Step 1: Identify the organisation's values and practices.
- Step 2: Identify the skills, knowledge and attitudes that link to this.
- Step 3: Define the scope and purpose of the evaluation.
- Step 4: Identify data sources and use a variety of sources.

Brinkerhoff (1987) also included two additional stages prior to the four existing levels, which he titled formative evaluation and summative evaluation.

Bushnell (1990) developed the IPO model (input, process, output) which, like the CIRO model, focuses more on the inputs to training. The IPO model is used by IBM and helps to monitor employee progress by setting performance indicators at each stage. The stages are:

- Input — such as the instructor experience, trainee qualifications, resources.
- Process — the plan, design, development and delivery of the training.
- Outputs — the trainees reactions, knowledge and skills gained and improved job performance.
- Outcomes — profits, customer satisfaction and productivity.

The outputs and outcomes stages of the model relate closely to Kirkpatrick's four levels.

Sleezer *et al.* (1992) developed Training Effectiveness Evaluation (TEE) which argues that an effective training course is one where the trainees and their managers are satisfied, the trainees learnt the content, they apply what they have learnt to their jobs and organisational performance is positively effected. The model differs little from Kirkpatrick, but does offer a comprehensive set of tools for measuring effectiveness. At the ultimate level it suggests the use of performance comparisons and/or cost-benefit analysis.

Fitz-enz (1994) developed a Training Valuation System (TVS) which is a four-step process similar to Kirkpatrick's framework at steps 3 and 4.

- Step 1: Situation analysis — this is similar to an in-depth training analysis. Like Kearns and Miller, he suggests that manager's answers are continuously probed until some visible, tangible outcome is revealed and that the questions initially focus on the work process rather than the training.

- Step 2: Intervention — this involves diagnosing the problem and designing the training.

- Step 3: Impact — this examines the variables that impact on performance.

- Step 4: Value — this step places a monetary worth on the changed performance.

For this process to work, he argues that there needs to be a strong partnership between the trainer and client/manager.

2.3 What do these models tell us?

Before going on to look at evaluation models that have moved substantially away from Kirkpatrick, it is worth comparing the models outlined above, which have Kirkpatrick's framework as their core. Table 2.1 aims to map the key elements of each model against the four levels of reaction, learning, behaviour and results.

Taken together, what appears is an expanded model which encapsulates certain elements both before assessing reactions and after an examination of organisational results.

The key elements cited before assessing reactions involve a broader analysis of the organisational context — its values, practices and current situation. Following this, there is a more explicit focus on the needs of the business and how these tie to the development of objectives and the design of the most appropriate solution. Whilst not forming part of the assessment process, it is argued that these contextual and training input steps inform the future evaluation strategy, and as such need to be included in any evaluation model.

Within the results level, there are suggestions that the benefits to the organisation should be made more explicit and focus on monetary values such as return on investment. The arguments for and against this are outlined later in Chapter 5. There may also be a need for evaluating beyond the organisation by examining the effects on the economy and society.

Table 2.1: Comparison of different models of training evaluation

Kirkpatrick	Hamblin	OEM Model	Indiana University	IS Carousel	Phillips, ROI	KPMT	CIRO
			Activity accounting	Identify business need; define development objective; design learning process		Staged process to examine the business needs; design solutions and get buy-in	Context analysis Input
Reaction	Reaction	Input process	Reaction	Experience the learning process	Reaction and planned action	Reaction to training and development	Reaction
Learning	Learning	Micro acquisition	Learning	Use and reinforce the learning	Learning	Learning	Outcome immediate
Behaviour	Job behaviour	Micro performance	Transfer of learning		Job application	Transfer to the workplace/ behaviour	Outcome intermediate
Results	Organisation	Macro	Business impact	Judge the benefits to the organisation	Business results	Bottom line added value	Outcome Ultimate
	Ultimate value	Mega Societal outcomes	Social impact		Return on Investment		

Source: IES, 2002

Many of the modifications to Kirkpatrick's existing levels differ by little more than semantics or interpretation. For example behaviour is perhaps more accurately described by the KPMT and Indiana University models as transfer of learning. Other useful additions include more detail on the different tools and techniques to employ at each level and the areas for analysis, as well as the need to work closer to the managers within the organisation and provide feedback of evaluation results.

3. Alternative Models

The literature on evaluation also provides some models of evaluation which have moved further away from Kirkpatrick. These loosely group into models that focus on the purpose of evaluation, and models that provide alternative measures.

3.1 Models focusing on the purpose of evaluation

3.1.1 Responsive evaluation: Pulley (1994)

Responsive evaluation is a tool for communicating evaluation results more effectively by tailoring it to the needs of the decision-makers. Pulley argues that the objective of the evaluation should be to provide evidence so that key decision-makers can determine what they want to know about the programme. The stages involved are:

1. Identify the decision-makers so as to ascertain who will be using the information and what their stake in it is.

2. Identify the information needs of the decision-makers — what do they need to know and how will it influence their decisions?

3. Systematically collect both quantitative and qualitative data. Pulley argues that the qualitative data is normally relayed in the form of stories or anecdotes and 'gives life to the numbers'.

4. Translate the data into meaningful information.

5. Involve and inform decision-makers on an on-going basis.

This technique has support from the literature. Abernathy (1999) states that you need to find out what your internal customers want to know about training and then collect the data that will answer those questions, rather than data defined by a pre-existing framework.

Bee and Bee (1994) also argue for clarity about the purpose of the evaluation. Some criteria, such as an examination of the quality of the trainer are sometimes made less explicit.

3.1.2 Educational evaluation: Stufflebeam *et al.* (1971)

This model, which was developed for evaluating in an educational context, distinguished four types of evaluation:

1. Context evaluation — which helps in planning and developing objectives.
2. Input evaluation — which helps to determine the design by examining capability, resources and different strategies.
3. Process evaluation — which helps to control the operations by providing on-going feedback.
4. Product evaluation — which helps to judge and react to the programme attainments in terms of outputs and outcomes.

They argue that process evaluation is essential to provide a basis for interpreting the reason for the outcome. There is a clear similarity between this and the CIRO model (Warr *et al.*, 1970) see section 2.2.7.

3.1.3 Newby (1992)

Newby's approach looks at the contexts of evaluation. He argues that you can evaluate within the training event, in the workplace after the event, in the context of performance measures, and finally using criteria not related to the workplace, such as societal, moral, political, or using philosophical criteria (such as an equal opportunities programme).

3.1.4 Evaluative enquiry — Preskill and Torres (1999)

Evaluative enquiry emphasises evaluation as a learning process. It connects evaluation to the organisation's mission and strategic plans, and emphasises that it is conducted within the context of learning for the organisation as a whole. *Evaluative Inquiry for Learning in Organizations* (EILO) emphasises:

- Addressing issues critical to an organisation's success.
- Dialogue, reflection and challenging assumptions.
- Program and organisational processes as well as outcomes.
- Opportunities for education and training of organisation practitioners in inquiry skills.
- Collaboration, co-operation, and participation.
- Using a diversity of perspectives to develop understanding about organisational issues.

3.2 Models using different measures

3.2.1 The learning outcomes approach: Kraiger *et al.* (1993)

This approach emphasises the importance of linking training evaluation to learning outcomes. From a set of training objectives they suggest the need to distinguish the three different types of outcomes — Cognitive, Skill-based and Affective and that this can be done by viewing the instructional objectives through different 'lenses'. The different perspectives look at the goals of training, the process strategies, and the performance criteria. By doing this they argue that the evaluation measures will become clearer.

3.2.2 The Balanced Scorecard: Kaplan and Norton (1996)

This process aims to balance business management by measuring across four different perspectives — finance, customers, internal business processes, and learning and growth. Kaplan and Norton suggest that measures of innovation and learning are as important as financial measures in evaluating a company's competitive position. However, the difficulty with this approach comes with selling the concept within the organisation (Spitzer, 1999).

3.2.3 Pay back: pay forward, CIPD, Lee (1994)

This approach, put forward by the CIPD, separates evaluation measures into pay back and pay forward results. Pay back describes the financial benefits, whereas pay forward means those benefits that flow from the training, which cannot be expressed directly in financial terms (indirect returns) — this ranges from impressionistic data from trainees to formal opinion surveys.

3.2.4 Concept Mapping and Pattern Matching: Anderson Consulting (Moad, 1995; Abernathy, 1999)

Anderson Consulting rejected the ROI model and the idea that business benefit from training could be isolated from other factors. They developed concept mapping and pattern matching, which is based on the premise that managers know the skills and behaviours needed by their employees, so stakeholder expectations are used to design and evaluate each course. It is based on market research techniques and seeks to map out expectations and match these with perceptions after the event.

3.3 Models for evaluating new technology delivery

There is widespread evidence from both organisational reports and academic literature of the increasing use of technology (in the form on online learning or eLearning) as part of a portfolio of training options available to HR managers. This does not mean to say that we have seen the end of instructor-led training (it still currently dominates the market with 70 per cent of all training — Pollard and Hillage 2001), nor would many suggest the replacement of all traditional learning methods. However, the share of instructor-led training in the market in the next few years is predicted to fall to about 35 to 40 per cent, to be overtaken by technology-based training (Pollard and Hillage 2001). Technology is therefore beginning to shape how training is delivered in organisations. Bassi and Cheney (1997) found a significant rise in the use of Internet and network-based electronic distance learning systems, in their benchmarking forum of 55 large multinationals. Organisations are exploring Web-based training, simulations, video conferenced training, videos, virtual environments, Internet and intranet courses *etc.*

A report from the IES Research Networks recently explored the world of eLearning, providing a summary of current research and practice (Pollard and Hillage 2001). It identified advantages and drawbacks of this form of learning within organisations, and raised a number of issues for managers and organisations to consider in taking forward any approach to eLearning. One of the key issues raised in the first review was 'How can you tell if it is working?'. Implementing an effective evaluation processes was identified as one of the main success factors for eLearning applications.

The reasons for evaluating technology-driven eLearning applications are similar to the reasons for evaluating any type of learning provisions. These might include:

- to determine whether the eLearning solution is accomplishing its objectives
- to identify who benefited the most or the least from the eLearning programme
- to identify areas for improvement.

However, in addition to this, the technology aspect of eLearning brings in other demands for evaluation. For example:

- The cost of technology often demands accountability, including measuring return on investment.
- The newness of eLearning to many participants brings pressure to develop information about its effectiveness and efficiency as a learning solution.
- Finally, because eLearning is not a proven process in many organisations, there is a need to show value now rather than later when it becomes a routine process.

Even with these strong imperatives, many HR managers may find that they either do not have time to evaluate, find it difficult to convince others of the importance of evaluation, or have enough difficulty getting the organisation to invest in the training, let alone the evaluation.

It is important to recognise that some of the processes used to evaluate other types of learning interventions will be applicable with eLearning. This often helps managers deal with the task of evaluation, in that it does not necessarily require a whole new set of skills and it might be easier than at first glance. Techniques for evaluating eLearning are broadly the same as evaluating other solutions. The data is the same (qualitative and quantitative) and the methods to isolate the effects of eLearning are the same. However, there are also some differences:

- The methods for collecting data at some levels of evaluation can be built into the process much more easily than traditional methods, for example in collecting reactions and examining learning online.
- Because eLearners can be remotely located, some of the traditional methods of data collection are more difficult to use, such as focus groups and direct observation.

At an organisational level of evaluation, eLearning is suggested to be cost effective, being cheaper to deliver than traditional classroom-based training. The actual reported amount varies, but studies in the EC and UK show cost savings of about one-third, with studies in the US being more generous. While this is an important piece of information for HR managers when going to the finance director or board to seek investment in eLearning projects, it is not the whole story for understanding the impact of such initiatives.

So what are the practices common to eLearning evaluation? Monitoring of learner progress is often put forward as a technique, which refers to the capabilities of the eLearning software to empower the training or learning administrators to track performance, and measure rates of return. Software can now be programmed to successfully monitor, assess and diagnose performance status (Salas and Cannon-Bowers, 2001). These researchers argue that the greatest challenge in evaluation is in designing, developing and testing on-line assessments of learning and performance. With computer-based training (CBT) becoming increasingly popular, Kraiger and Jung (in Quinones, 1997) argue that intelligent tutoring systems (ITS) and hyper-test or hypermedia training (HMT) will make the process of designing evaluation measures easier. However, they state that for both systems it may be helpful to assess trainees' understanding of system functioning as well as training content. A further element in many eLearning systems is behaviour and usage analysis. This is the ability to automatically generate information on how much any individual uses a system.

It has been suggested that evaluation has an advantage within eLearning. It is often hard to measure the overall effectiveness of traditional training because it is difficult either to verify that the training has been completed, or the extent to which the information given has been understood. With eLearning, tracking of learner performance and certification can overcome this.

In the recent report on eLearning produced by IES (Pollard and Hillage 2001), the evidence indicated that best practice organisations were focusing eLearning evaluations on measuring performance, competencies and intellectual capital (Hall and LeCavalier, 2000). The most successful of these focused their evaluations on job performance measures using web-enabled competency management systems. The focus has therefore shifted away from testing for the sake of it, to a more sophisticated analysis of linking learning objectives to outcomes, while providing relevant and timely feedback.

This shift in focus is necessary and timely, as the content of eLearning changes over the next few years. Much of the current content of eLearning initiatives has tended to fall into the delivery of IT skills and training. This accounts for $0.87 billion of the training spend in the US, four times larger than the soft skills sector of the market. It also dominates in the UK. The business and soft skills section of the market is much smaller, but is growing and is predicted to surpass IT online training by 2003 (Pollard and Hillage 2001). As organisations move away from IT skills to delivering more complex skills via eLearning, a broader set of evaluation methodologies will be required. Understanding and embracing some of these methodologies is likely to be the major challenge for those charged with eLearning initiatives.

Sloman (2001) argues that eLearning will be most effective for the acquisition of knowledge and least effective where interpersonal interactions are needed. He expresses concern that eLearning will pose critical issues about the time individuals put aside for learning. This ability to learn at any time may also impact on evaluation and how it is carried out. Salmon (2001) has already found in his research that e-moderators for educational learning cannot be online 24 hours a day to evaluate what's happening, and so other methods and systems must be in place to evaluate progress.

3.4 What do these alternative models tell us?

Models in the first group clearly indicate that there is a need to identify the reasons for the evaluation, and that the tools and techniques employed will alter depending on why the evaluation is taking place and who it is for. Pulley's model of responsive evaluation in particular, emphasises the importance of tailoring the evaluation strategy to the audience within the organisation, rather than putting measures in place for the sake of it.

Models in the second group indicate that there is a need to focus more clearly on the different types of outcomes sought by the training and development activity, and to tailor the technique to the organisation in order to ensure that the approach suits the culture and values. In addition, there is an increased emphasis on non-financial measures and a suggestion that a more rounded picture needs to be developed to show the indirect returns on all aspects of the business.

With a growing demand for eLearning it is clear that systems have the ability to take away some of the routine evaluation and assessments from training staff, and track progress. However, it is likely that new issues will arise and the aspects requiring evaluation may well be different to those for conventional training.

4. A Model of Development

All of the models of evaluation tacitly base themselves on an assumption that there is a chain of impact from a development event or process to individual learning and to organisational/societal impact. In effect, these models assume an underlying model of learning. Indeed, some of the criticism levelled at the Kirkpatrick model is because of confusion around whether it is a model or taxonomy of training evaluation, the training process or of learning.

- Several have criticised the fact that the Kirkpatrick model commences after the training or development event has occurred and therefore cannot fully take into account the design of the development event.

- Many comments focus on the lack of a grounding of training and development to the business plan, *ie* the four-level model does not take fully into account the original business need. Many have been very outspoken that all training should be based on business need and all evaluation should be related to business outcome.

Such criticisms, whilst debating the range of the model and suggesting some broadening to include identification of development need and the means by which development is delivered, have not fundamentally challenged the detail of the model itself. Others have raised more fundamental objections:

- A number have questioned the underlying assumption that there is a linear relationship between reaction, learning, application, and organisational impact. The model ignores many of the intervening variables that determine the interrelationships, such as:

- motivation to learn, *ie* learning readiness, job attitudes, personality characteristics, and motivation to transfer

- performance outcomes, including the motivation to transfer, and job attitudes

- transfer conditions, *ie* support, transfer design, goal setting and practice.

● Some have questioned whether trainee reaction has any relationship to learning outcomes. There is some statistical evidence that it does not, whereas others have found relationships between reactions and learning.

In some ways, the criticisms of the Kirkpatrick model are unfair, in that it is a model for training evaluation rather than a model of the training or learning system. It focuses on a range of responses to learning from the most immediate to the most distant. Other models that have extended the Kirkpatrick framework, have perhaps muddled the debate by mixing an evaluative framework with elements of a model of the learning process. They include elements of design and ways in which development needs are determined.

Before we go on to look in more detail at some of the evidence available from the literature on such a model of learning and measuring impact at different stages, we explore in this chapter what such a model might look like. A process model of development should take into account a wide range of factors that are instrumental in the ability of learning and development processes to result in organisational outcomes. Although evaluation needs to be underpinned by a model of development, it does not have to match such a model exactly; it may well be a simplification or it may be less inclusive. The degree to which it is desirable to measure all aspects is dependent on the circumstances of the evaluation, and issues such as the time, money and resources available.

4.1 A model of learning

Conceptualising learning and development as a process helps the evaluation, as the successful implementation will depend on all the stages being in place. A model of learning tries to articulate how a training or development event is translated into observable differences within organisations or other social settings. A model makes the steps in that process explicit, and thereby helps design and apply evaluation. Many of the models of evaluation we have looked at implicitly build on an underlying model of learning with their evaluation of certain key stages.

4.1.1 Inputs to learning

Learning does not take place in a vacuum but is dependent on a correct identification of learning need. Learning need can be individual or organisational and may arise from the business plan, environmental considerations, or a personal development plan.

In terms of expressing need, it is important to also think more widely than the business plan. This may not be clear on the implications for people and may have missed some important pressures on the organisation that may give rise to development needs. Determining organisational need (see Figure 4.1) may require multiple perspectives: the business plan; an awareness of environmental pressure; and the views of those in the organisation.

Individuals' learning needs will similarly be influenced by previous learning and other experiences, role, and changes in their environment.

Figure 4.1: Organisational inputs to learning

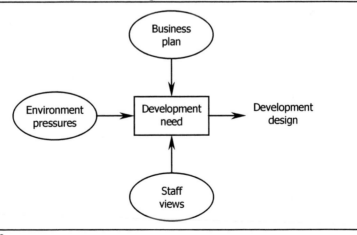

Source: IES, 2002

4.1.2 Learning process

Having identified need, the next stage is the delivery of a learning event, whether that is a formal training/development event or an informal learning opportunity. Other considerations in the delivery of the event include all the aspects of quality, appropriateness of methods used, amount of time spent *etc.*, that will influence learning outcomes. There is evidence that how you learn will influence what you learn (Tamkin *et al.* 1998, Mumford 1997) with action learning and other methods emphasising reflection, being more likely to lead to insight.

Another key consideration in terms of the evaluation process, but one which is generally overlooked, is to understand what aspect of human performance the learning is intended to affect. This will help determine what kinds of learning process might be expected to be successful, and the tools for evaluation.

There is evidence that different kinds of learning lead to different learning outcomes and therefore, when planning an event and delivering it, the process used should match the desired objectives for the event. For example, previous research at IES (Tamkin and Barber, 1998) suggests that formal learning that is about 'out there' (*ie* organisational design, business strategy, HR systems) is more likely to lead to external knowledge and skill acquisition than learning events that are informal and about what is 'in here' (*ie* personal skills, attitudes and attributes). Such internally focused events are also more likely to lead to insight, creativity *etc.*, and therefore we should be aware of such linkages when evaluating the impact of training and development events. In thinking about the aspects of human performance, it might be useful to consider three domains of experience:

- Heart — *ie values, personality and attitudes*
- Mind — *ie knowledge*
- Body — *ie skills*

In fact these might be thought of as layers of human attributes, with the innermost layers being the most firmly embedded and the most difficult to change (see Figure 4.2). The deeper into these layers the training/development is intended to affect, the more personal the learning experience and the more qualitative the evaluation tools.

Figure 4.2: Domains of human performance

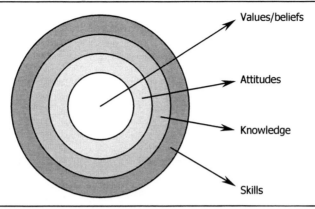

Values/beliefs

Attitudes

Knowledge

Skills

Source: IES, 2002

4.1.3 Transfer conditions

Whether an event does actually lead to an individual applying the learning will depend on a number of other factors that are independent of the quality or appropriateness of the event itself. Such individual factors include attitude to work, and motivation to transfer (which may relate to belief in positive outcomes from transfer), organisational factors (which will include the freedom to apply the learning, the impact of organisational culture, the support to the learner in the transfer stage, the numbers of individuals having undertaken a specific event *etc.*).

4.1.4 Organisational outcomes

Even if the learning is successfully applied in the workplace, there is still an issue as to whether the learning impacts noticeably on the organisation. The kind of impact that might be expected is obviously related to the original learning need. For learning to spread beyond the individual, it needs to be maintained over time, and may also take some time for outcomes to be achieved. In work on the impact of Investors in People; Tamkin and Hillage (1998) showed that there was a chain of impact that took some time to develop. Organisational impact will also depend on the numbers of individuals who have experienced the learning event and made successful learning transfer to the job, and their position within the organisation.

Figure 4.3: A model of learning

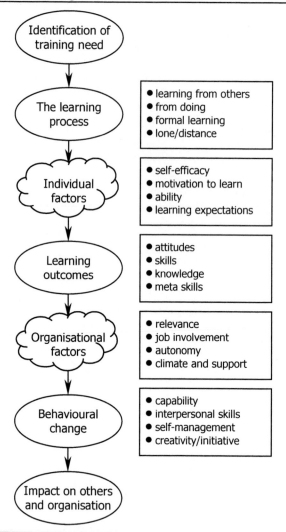

Source: IES, 1995

These various stages are shown in the model of learning (Figure 4.3). This assumes a chain of impact from a learning event to learning, from learning to changed behaviour, and from changed behaviour to impact on others, the organisation in general and beyond. It recognises that there are mediating factors that will affect the strength of the relationship between one link in the chain and another.

4.2 A model of evaluation

A model of the evaluation process is not the same as developing a model of the learning process. It exists to support practitioners apply the practice of evaluation more coherently than they might otherwise. It provides structure to the evaluation process and can suggest methods and means of doing so. It is of necessity a simplification and takes into account the reality of resources (including time, money, information and expertise) available to organisations.

The model below (Figure 4.4), follows the primary route of the development model, but does not spell out all the intervening variables that may affect development. The inclusion of such other variables is dependent on the individual evaluation and is

Figure 4.4: A model of evaluation

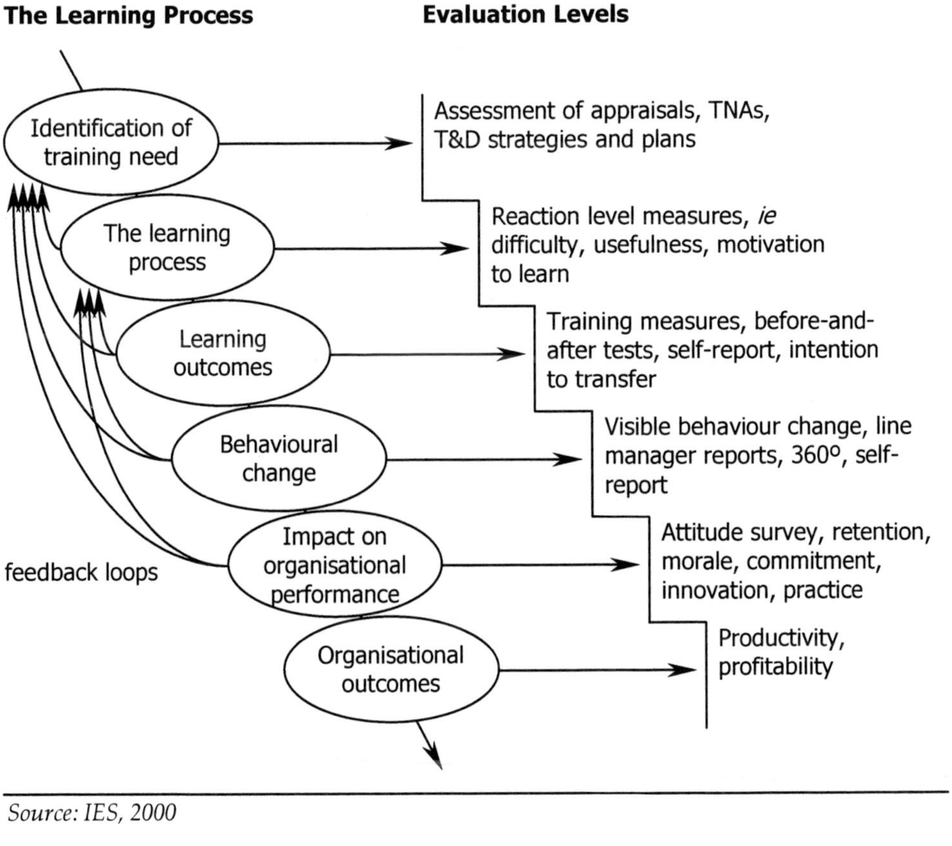

The Learning Process   **Evaluation Levels**

- Identification of training need → Assessment of appraisals, TNAs, T&D strategies and plans
- The learning process → Reaction level measures, *ie* difficulty, usefulness, motivation to learn
- Learning outcomes → Training measures, before-and-after tests, self-report, intention to transfer
- Behavioural change → Visible behaviour change, line manager reports, 360°, self-report
- Impact on organisational performance → Attitude survey, retention, morale, commitment, innovation, practice
- Organisational outcomes → Productivity, profitability

feedback loops

Source: IES, 2000

likely to be dependent on the importance of the original development need, the cost of the development programme and the complexity of the learning process. Because such intervening variables are likely to add to the complexity and the cost of the evaluation, they are more likely to be important if the initial evaluation has shown that there are problems with outcome. In any large scale evaluation some of the factors may not be as critical as others; individual motivation to learn may not be a critical intervening variable where there are many participants.

The model shows how evaluation results can feed back to provide information on the design or the delivery of the training event. The model starts before the event itself. As much of the literature stresses, it begins with the articulation of an organisational or individual need. Many commentators insist that this need should be embedded in the business plan, but it could just as easily be the articulation of environmental pressures or of some future scenario planning (see Figure 4.1). With an effective appraisal or personal development planning scheme, it should also be possible to root all individual development needs back to a job/role, and therefore related to an organisational need. Nonetheless, some individuals will have development needs that may not be directly related to the business plan, or that they do not necessarily share with the organisation, and that may, or may not, be expressed in their personal development plan.

Our model of the evaluation process can now be used to underpin an exploration of the literature that is relevant to the key stages of:

- reactions to the learning event
- learning
- changing behaviour
- organisational impact.

5. Evaluating at Different Levels

Aside from the research into new models of evaluation since Kirkpatrick, there is another body of literature which provides information on some of the issues governing the effectiveness of evaluating at each of the four levels of reactions, learning, behaviour and results. The lessons which can be learnt from examining this literature help to inform the debate as to the value of the different models put forward.

5.1 Reactions

The purpose of evaluating at the reaction level is primarily to assess what the participants initially thought and felt about the training and development programme. A recent study by the Industrial Society found that 84 per cent of companies evaluate reactions using end of course reaction questionnaires or 'reactionnaires' (Industrial Society, 2000). Yet despite this, there is also considerable evidence to suggest that reaction-level evaluation has little value.

Kirkpatrick (1983) argues that evaluating reactions is crucial, as the organisation wants the customers (participants) to come back to future programmes and recommend them to others. He purports that 'unhappy customers will probably not learn very much'. Bee and Bee (1994) agree and add that comments on the general content, methods and pitch can be particularly useful in the early stages of the training programme's life.

However, Warr *et al.* (1999) found that although participant reactions were related to learning, they were generally unrelated to subsequent job behaviour. They examined reactions on three dimensions — the enjoyment of the training, perceptions of its usefulness, and its perceived difficulty (which was negatively related to learning). This finding of poor correlation between reactions and learning, is backed up by other researchers, who also found that humour in training in particular, did not lead to higher levels of learning, to the extent that negative relationships between reactions and learning were found in educational research (Alliger and Janak, 1989).

One reason for this may be that learners often mistake good presentation style for good learning and difficult messages may lead to poor ratings. Psychologists have argued that people are not good at reporting their experiences of learning (Alliger and Janak, 1989) and suggest that only when trainees are experiencing the training as unpleasant do they start to learn. Ghodsian *et al.* (1997) argue against trainees evaluating training instructors for this reason, as the evaluation data may lead to inappropriate changes to the training programme.

Holton (1996) also argues against using reactions as an outcome of training. He drew on numerous research studies to show that there is little correlation between reactions and learning. He even went so far as to argue that they should be removed from evaluation models, particularly when the reaction measures focus on enjoyment.

However, there is still some confusion over the causal relationships among variables, and it is not at all clear whether lower level categories can predict higher level measures. Bassi *et al.* (Blanchard *et al.* 2000) found that reaction measures had some predictive validity for behavioural and results measures. Clement (1982) also found a significant relationship between reaction and learning when testing Hamblin's hierarchy. However, many other studies fail to find positive relationships. One reason for this may be due to the lack of sophistication of performance measures such as behavioural rating scales, which may not be sensitive enough to pick up differences stemming from training. Another possible reason could be due to the nature of the reactions being analysed. Lee and Pershing (1999) in their studies, classified eleven dimensions of reaction level evaluation, and give advice on the design and development of reactionnaires.

Due to the ease with which companies can issue and analyse reactionnaires, their widespread use is perhaps not surprising. However, Dawson (1995) suggests that using reactionnaires has become a ritual and that sheets used at the end of a course need to be more specific and aimed at improving the course process. Questions should include the pace of the course, sequencing, training aids and administration. To determine whether objectives have been met she recommends tailoring the sheets to each course more effectively. She also argues that learning a truth about oneself may be uncomfortable and warns against happiness ratings which show how people felt about the course.

Taken together, the literature suggests that companies need to analyse more carefully the types of reactions they need to assess, and be clear about the purpose of this data. If organisations are seeking to evaluate the *value* of training rather than aiming to improve on its content, then reaction data may not be appropriate. The evidence is mixed and suggests a complex relationship between immediate response to an event and learning gain, and even less between reactions and behaviour change. In some ways this is illustrative of a general problem with all HR interventions. The further one travels along the chain of impact, so the benefits of the intervention diminish and become more difficult to measure.

To some extent, this debate relates to the different definitions of evaluation. Many writers on the subject now differentiate between *training* validation, which is concerned with whether the training and development achieved what it set out to do, and *training evaluation,* which focuses on the impact of that training and development. However, even when there is an interest in improving training effectiveness, by validating the training content and process, the literature suggests that data generated need to be treated with caution, due to the inability of trainees to distinguish learning from style.

5.2 Learning

Evaluation at a learning level provides data on the degree of change to knowledge, skills or attitude stemming from the programme, and is normally assessed using some type of performance tests, or by participant and line manager feedback on the extent of learning that has taken place.

There is a high level of agreement in the literature that, ideally, measures of performance need to be taken both before and after the training event, to be able to assess gains in learning. Methods for testing learning have become quite sophisticated, with techniques such as criterion-referenced testing (Shrock and Coscarelli, 1989). Control groups are also commonly suggested as a good way of countering the effects of other factors which may affect performance levels, but in reality, large-scale testing prior to training, and establishing control groups, are not practical for organisations due to the numbers involved and organisational constraints. As a result, the measures actually used are often less rigorous.

Increasingly, organisations are using testing as part of the training programme itself, due to practical access difficulties and resistance from organisations to post-training assessment. Testing during training is seen as valuable in not only providing a measure, but also helping individuals recall information more easily in the future. Most tests administered during training aim to test retention, but Ghodsian *et al.* (1997) argue that transfer tests, which assess the likely transfer of learning, can also be set by using scenarios taken from the workplace.

Erikson (1990) distinguishes between operational knowledge and theoretical knowledge. He argues that a trainee can repeat theories, giving the appearance of learning, but may be unable to apply it. Consequently, testing learning without putting it in context will not show the value.

Others also suggest that assessing learning during training needs to be undertaken with care. Ghodsian *et al.* (1997) state that trainees' performance during training is an unreliable predictor of post-training performance. For example, it has been found that massing skills practice on courses can result in rapid improvement and high levels of performance during the training, but little learning is actually achieved, as learners are prevented from making mistakes and learning from them. The studies found that variable practice — *ie* using different tasks, is more beneficial than constant (same task) practice in aiding the future transfer of learning. Despite this, the fact that trainers are often assessed on the performance of trainees at the end of a course may lead trainers to increase short-term performance over long-term learning.

There are situations however, where comprehensive evaluations at this level may not be necessary, such as when the trainees are aiming to achieve a required standard or level of competence. For example, Sackett and Mullen (1993) argue that where the training is simply aimed at achieving a certain level of performance, post-test-only measures, with no control groups or pre-testing, are perfectly adequate. Some researchers also argue against evaluating at a learning level for other types of programme. Rough (1994) argues that some soft skills and values (such as integrity or caring) are not learnt in a linear fashion, but require a breakthrough to new levels of understanding about ways of being. He argues that these need to be taught in a transformational way, where trainees discover things for themselves, and that testing learning can limit transformational change. He cites an example of testing original thinking — which by the act of setting measures for what is original, will limit the creativity that can be measured. With transformational change there is often a period of frustration and resistance, which can be a sign that people are beginning to recognise the issue — thus reaction measures and learning tests are likely to be a poor indicator of success. Other research by IES (Tamkin *et al.*, 1998) has indicated that skills and knowledge may be of two distinct kinds: that which is 'out there', *ie* of the external world, and that which is 'in here', of the internal world of the individual (see Figure 5.1). Internal knowledge is about self, personal strengths and weaknesses, and internal skills are the strategies to work with these. Transformational processes work at the internal level and do not lend themselves to testing.

Bee and Bee (1994) outline the advantages and disadvantages of various assessment methods at this level. They point out that assessing skills is far more resource intensive than assessing knowledge, as typically it requires a pool of trained observers. Due to this, pre-evaluations of skills are often rare. 360 degree assessment is growing in popularity in organisations and is one way of assessing competency gains over time. Motorola, for example, used 360-degree performance appraisal to measure leadership behaviours and looked at how this relates to training received (Blanchard *et al.*, 2000).

As we have already noted, there is general consensus in the evaluation models that the learning objectives need to be made clear before the start of a training programme, in order to be able

Figure 5.1: External and internal skills and knowledge

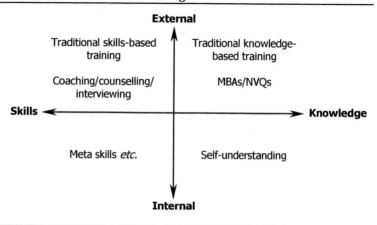

Source: Bourner, 1998

to assess the learning gains. Newby (1992) supports the need for well-defined training objectives, and states that they should incorporate:

- the behaviour to be demonstrated after the training
- the standard of performance to be attained
- the conditions under which performance is to occur.

However, he also argues that there are some training purposes which do not depend on measuring the objectives themselves:

- where personal objectives legitimately differ from organisational ones
- where the interest concerns the process of learning rather than the outcomes
- to ensure that unanticipated effects are picked up on — *ie* unanticipated spin-offs.

It is clear from the literature that whilst in-depth evaluations using pre- and post-testing alongside control groups are possible, in many organisations the rigour of thorough evaluation is unattainable. Indeed, it could even be argued that for more transformational programmes, this type of evaluation is not even appropriate. Newby argues that practitioners need to work with their constraints and opportunities to use evaluation tools to best effect. It is important to clarify why the information is being collected and what use will be made of it. Different types of evaluation can then be used, depending on the nature, scope and purposes of evaluating the training programme. Where knowledge testing takes place within training, it is suggested that practical scenarios will be more valuable than purely testing theory.

5.3 Behaviour and the transfer of learning

There are concerns that much of the training taking place in organisations fails to transfer to the work setting. In response to this, there is a wealth of research into the factors that predict training effectiveness. Kraiger *et al.* (1993), Axtell *et al.* (1997), Holton (1996) and Kraiger and Aguinis (2001) all provide reviews of the situational and individual factors that affect both learning and post-training outcomes. These loosely group into variables related to the organisation, individual variables, and variables in the training itself.

5.3.1 Organisational factors

The organisational climate and level of managerial support

The transfer climate and the organisation's culture have been shown to have significant effects on the transfer of learning on programmes, to changed behaviour in the workplace (Tracey, Tannenbaum and Kavanagh, 1995). Research indicates that when supervisors and peers encourage and reward the application of course material, the training is likely to achieve more positive results. Warr *et al.* (1999) also found that changes in job behaviour were predicted by the transfer climate and learning confidence. In particular, the perceived difficulty of the training was strongly negatively predictive, and the level of support from managers subsequently, strongly positively predictive of future application of skills and knowledge.

The period of time immediately after the training event has also been found to be critical in aiding transfer of learning to the workplace. During these initial phases, errors are more likely to occur and reinforcement and support from managers is essential (Axtell *et al.*, 1997). It is suggested that providing trainees with training-related goals to be attained in the first month back at work, would help to maximise the level of transfer.

The relevance or usefulness of the course to the person's job

The degree to which a person's expectations about the training are met has a significant impact on post-training attitudes and motivation to transfer learning (Holton, 1996).

Job Involvement

People with higher commitment to their jobs are more likely to perceive rewards from transferring learning (Holton, 1996).

The level of autonomy in the job

People with more autonomous jobs have more scope to apply the learning without being constrained by their manager or peers.

5.3.2 Individual factors

Trainees may well be embarking on a given training activity from different starting points, because of their personality or motivation, for example. This level of motivation, and belief about own capability, are undoubtedly going to influence the learning process. Research has demonstrated that individual factors and other variables are likely to have a significant impact on the learning process. As such, they ideally need to be evaluated prior to the learning activity. Change in such characteristics may also be an outcome of the training activity itself (*eg* increased motivation post training delivery) and so measurement can provide multiple indicators.

Self-efficacy

Research has shown for example that an individual's 'self-efficacy', or the degree to which trainees have confidence in their own ability to cope with the learning task, is a strong predictor of learning levels during training and subsequent outcomes. Employees high in self-efficacy are more likely to seek out opportunities to apply new skills. Salas and Cannon-Bowers

(2001) suggest it may be worth considering self-efficacy as a deliberate training intervention (*ie* aiming to raise self-efficacy level) as well as an indicator of training success. Positive feedback for example, can increase self-efficacy levels.

Motivation

Trainees' motivation to learn and attend training has a significant effect on their skill acquisition, retention and willingness to put the new skills and knowledge into practice (Salas and Cannon-Bowers, 2001). Holton (1996) divides motivation into the individual's readiness for the training, their attitudes to their job, personality characteristics, and motivation to transfer learning. Where trainees have a choice in training content, where they are more committed to their job, and where they have a need to achieve, they have been found to be more motivated.

Kraiger and Aguinis (2001) argue that mandatory training often suffers due to the impact it has on employee motivation.

Ability

General intelligence has been found to promote self-efficacy and performance (Salas and Cannon-Bowers, 2001; Holton, 1996) and hence more able trainees apply more learning.

5.3.3 Training factors

Goal setting

The arguments for goal setting are mixed. Some research has found that individuals who set specific goals are more likely to transfer the learning into behaviours on the job (Gist *et al*, 1990; Holton, 1996) whilst others found the results inconclusive (Wexley and Baldwin, 1986).

5.3.4 Measuring intervening factors

The case

Given that these variables have been shown to have a significant effect on the transfer of learning to behaviour, it could be argued that measures for these variables should be built into any evaluation. Holton (1996) for example, suggests including self-reports to collect data on variables such as management support, personal characteristics and motivation. However, Falletta (1998) argues that: 'If organisations are incapable of implementing a simple four-level evaluation framework, they are not likely to understand or use an empirically tested, integrative causal model.' Certainly, the literature reporting evaluation studies that have incorporated intervening variables, have been highly complex, academic studies which are unlikely to be suited to most organisations.

However, the research into the influences on training effectiveness can provide some useful insights into how to design training events to maximise learning benefits. For example, to maximise the transfer of learning it would be beneficial to:

- ensure management support for participants
- establish short-term and long-term goals for participants
- increase the level of self-efficacy using positive feedback
- allow participants to influence the content of the programme
- ensure that expectations are explicit and aim to fulfil these.

The practice

Evaluating changes in behaviour following training and development entails measuring the degree to which the learning on the programme is being applied. There are a number of different measures which can be used to do this, each of which has limitations.

Self-assessment

The most common methods of assessment are manager assessment and self-assessment in the workplace. Bee and Bee (1994) outline the pros and cons of each and point out that the ability and willingness of individuals to self-assess honestly and accurately is questionable. This is echoed by Carless and Roberts-Thompson (2001) who studied self-ratings of performance for 545 participants on an Airforce Officer training programme. They found that self-ratings did not correspond well with peer and training staff ratings, and that poor performers in particular were unable to predict their performance accurately. Ostroff (1991) argues that frequently-used measures such as behaviour and performance rating scales may not be sensitive enough to detect training effects.

Noonan and Sulsky (2001) found that the accuracy of behavioural ratings increased dramatically when behavioural observation training had taken place. They argue that due to the costs and time implications of training, common frames of reference for observers could also come from case studies and discussion. However, observation as a measurement method may raise concerns over validity, as observation can lead employees to alter their performance (Twitchell *et al.*, 2000).

Timing of evaluation

The issue of when to measure behavioural change will vary, depending on the nature of the training. Kirkpatrick (1983) suggests a post-training appraisal three months or more after the training, although he recognises that some participants may not change their behaviour for six months, or may change before regressing to previous behaviours. However, a study by Axtell *et al.* (1997) showed that the amount of learning transferred after one month was a strong predictor of the amount transferred after a year, indicating that using both measures may not be necessary.

As with learning measures, ideally the appraisal of performance should be made before and after the training event and if practical, control groups (not receiving the training) should be used as comparators.

Bee and Bee (1994) state that behavioural evaluation is potentially the most valuable source of information for assessing training. They argue that to do this effectively it is essential to secure the co-operation of managers and trainees, and aim to minimise the impact on the workplace. This leads to the question of who should carry out the evaluation at this level.

Who should evaluate?

Lack of line manager support for evaluation was cited by 42 per cent of the Industrial Society's research (2000) as one of the most common problems in training evaluation, and is particularly critical when evaluating beyond levels 1 and 2. Rae (1999) argues that training departments need to educate line managers about their role in evaluation. She argues that line managers are the best people to follow through post-event, by discussing action plans and supporting implementation of goals. By doing this they will have a greater understanding of the value that can be fed into any analysis.

One means of engaging with the line more fully is to work with them. A decade ago, Newby (1992) stated that 'one option for people with a responsibility for training is to move towards becoming an internal consultant, who plays a more active part in shaping policy issues and long-term organisational change'. Spitzer (1999) later argued similarly, that evaluators need to work as 'real partners' with other managers in the organisation to gain a greater understanding of the performance measures and causal links.

Interestingly, Twitchell *et al.* (2000) found that where the training staff were more highly trained or experienced, it was more likely that level 3 or 4 evaluation would take place.

5.4 Results

It is universally agreed that evaluation at the behavioural and results levels are made more difficult due to the fact that training is not the only relevant causal factor. The further one attempts to measure the impact from the training event itself, the greater the difficulty in attributing cause and effect. Despite this, the literature suggests that there is an increasing concern in organisations to justify the investment in training in terms of improved organisational performance, such as increased productivity, profit or safety, reduced error and enhanced market share.

As can be seen from the earlier models of evaluation, there are a number of supporters of the view that results can and should be analysed using numerical 'hard' data. Spitzer (1999) sums up the view that all results can be turned into numerical measures, stating that 'every business has hundreds and thousands of intermediate indicators of organisational effectiveness: manufacturing efficiency, inventory levels, accidents, order-entry accuracy, abandoned calls, defect rates, cycle times — all these things measure real business results'.

Plenty of guidance is also available for practitioners on measuring productivity (Brinkerhoff and Dressler, 1990), cost-effectiveness (Levin, 1983), and return on investment (Phillips, 1996, Kearns and Miller, 1997). The argument that gathering hard data is not always possible is dismissed by these researchers. Newby (1992) differentiates between cost-benefit analysis and cost effectiveness analysis, where the costs can be specified but the training outcomes, though identifiable, do not have an obvious monetary value. He argues that even then, managers can be asked to put a cash value on many benefits. Kearns and Miller (1997) also argue that the objectives should be clearly defined so that they spell out the financial implications.

Holton (1996) concurs that interventions not linked to organisational mission, strategy and goals are unlikely to produce results that are valued by the organisation. He also argues that the financial benefits should be forecast before the intervention begins, as individuals will be more motivated if they can see the value.

Many writers on the subject talk about gathering evidence instead of proof, and Bee and Bee (1994) suggest taking a pragmatic rather than a perfectionist view about what can be assessed. They argue that all cost/benefit analyses are littered with assumptions of some sort, but if these are explicit then it is possible to find some evidence.

However, the process of linking training to business results is highly interpretative, especially in complex business environments. Pulley (1994) argues that what is needed is 'responsive evaluation' which pays attention to both hard and soft issues and provides both quantitative and qualitative measures. She states that relying too heavily on either type of data can result in misleading conclusions. She draws on research which shows that people's actions tend to be more affected by stories and anecdotes than statistical results, and argues that although senior managers may request hard data, they are more influenced by qualitative measures.

Indeed, there are a considerable number of researchers that argue against using financial data to analyse results. Abernathy (1999) stated 'I don't believe that level 4 is applicable to soft skills training. There are too many variables that can impact performance, other than the training itself.' Alliger and Janak

(1989) also cite an example where a plant manager argued against a quantitative evaluation on the basis that it prevented the idea of the intervention being kept at the forefront of people's minds. Nickols (2000) also argues against hard measures and states that as the goals of training are generally to prevent mistakes, errors or waste, rather than correct them, the true measure of training probably lies in its absence rather than its presence.

The ability of 'hard' measures to become visible in an appropriate time-frame is also questioned. Newby, for example, argues that organisational constraints impact on the rigor of evaluation, and that whilst some measures and cross-validation can be achieved, the 'worth' of a programme is not just about cost-benefit. His experience suggests that it can take 12 to 18 months to establish evaluation data that prove the effectiveness of training, and that the time lag needs to be taken into account when relating results to the bottom line. Kaplan and Norton (1996) go further than this, and argue that financial measures are inadequate for guiding and evaluating organisations. 'They are lagging indicators that fail to capture much of the value that has been created or destroyed by manager's actions in the accounting period.'

In addition, some transformational programmes aimed at shifting culture can often happen before the organisation is ready for them, and consequently the benefits are not visible for some time. Rough (1994) argues that progress sometimes needs to be based upon trust, mutual involvement and facilitation.

The Ministry of Defence evaluation toolkit (July 2001) states that evidence of results can be direct, indirect, quantifiable or qualitative, as long as managers have a sufficient range of information with which to make a decision. It would appear that the need to provide results in financial terms will vary according to the purpose of the training and the audience for the evaluation. According to Tamkin and Hillage (1997), employers provide training and development for one of three main reasons:

- Vision: a belief in the value of development as an investment in people
- Utility: to create greater efficiency and quality of service or product
- Culture: to impact on the individual's loyalty, self-respect and self-esteem.

Where the purpose is a visionary or cultural one in particular, it could be argued that qualitative data is needed to provide a rounded picture of the impact on the business. Lee and Pershing (2000) also question whether there are other perspectives — such as strategic alignment or adaptability to change, that may be more pertinent for organisational effectiveness in today's economy. They argue that many of the assessments focus on individuals as the unit of analysis, whereas evaluation of teams or departments may be more appropriate.

Demonstrating a linkage between development activity and organisational outcomes might be akin to searching for the holy grail. Certainly, hard evidence of such linkages are rare in the literature, even with the resources of academic researchers to design and conduct rigorous evaluation studies. The data demands of such an evaluation would defeat most organisations' data systems, and the rigour of analysis exceed the evaluation skills of most trainers and HR experts. The fact that so few organisations actually evaluate at level four, despite the urging of many, is probably testimony enough to its complexity.

We now turn to look at the evidence of how organisations have responded.

6. The Lessons for Practice

6.1 Current activity

The Industrial Society's (2000) study of 487 Personnel and HR specialists found that 84 per cent use end of course questionnaires and 35 per cent some derivation of the Kirkpatrick model. Two-thirds of the sample said that the amount of evaluation had grown in the last two years and 84 per cent stated that it was likely to grow in the next two years.

Older surveys generally point to less activity. The training in Britain survey (Deloitte, Haskins and Sells, 1989) estimated that only 19 per cent of organisations tried to evaluate the benefits of training, and only three per cent of those attempted cost/benefit analysis. A further survey of large companies in Britain (Marginson *et al*, 1993) showed that only 13 per cent of firms evaluated their training effort.

One of the reasons for this growth is Investors in People. The fourth principle of IiP is evaluation of the business benefits from investment in training and development. IiP is a total quality framework and works on the premise that evaluation sits in a cycle of planning, doing, evaluating and reviewing. However, there is limited guidance on evaluation methodologies. The need to evaluate as part of the IiP standard has had a significant effect, and 45 per cent of organisations cite this as a prime reason for carrying out evaluation (Industrial Society, 2000).

The 1997 ASTD benchmarking forum (Bassi and Cheney, 1997) found that Kirkpatrick's model is still the predominant means of evaluating training, with over 50 per cent of companies reporting its use. It also found that whilst more companies were evaluating at levels 3 and 4, the overall percentage of courses evaluated at those levels had not increased. This suggests that organisations are becoming more strategic about using such tools.

Twitchell *et al.* (2000) analysed various survey sources and concluded that the general patterns are the same. Many organisations use level 1 and 2 for at least some programmes; fewer than half even try level 3, and only a small percentage employ level 4 evaluation. Even where the training is more technical and supposedly more straightforward to evaluate, there is little variation to this. Plant and Ryan (1994) in their study of 72 companies in the South of England with over 300 employees, also found that the main method of evaluation is by student reaction, and debriefing between managers and participants.

So is the suggestion that organisations are being forced to focus more on financial returns to the business valid? Blanchard *et al.* (2000) found that none of the companies with comprehensive training evaluation such as IBM, Motorola and Arthur Anderson, evaluated in order to justify training or maintain a training budget, but did so in response to customer needs. This view is supported by Twitchell *et al.* (2000) who found that the most commonly reported reason for not evaluating was that it was not required by the organisation. Some larger companies may not appear to be evaluating at all, as they do so as part of a total HR system rather than for training specifically. General Electric, for example, uses surveys to realign training, but the emphasis is on quality measures to improve delivery rather than on measurement of outcomes.

However, there is some evidence of higher level evaluations taking place. British Telecom (Bee and Bee, 1994) carried out a study to determine the financial worth of some of their training. They used critical incident interviews with line managers to determine failure costs due to poor performance by junior managers. BT's 7 million pound investment in training was estimated to have brought a 280 million pound return to the company over a six year period, although arriving at this figure involved some major assumptions being made.

There also appears to be a greater shift towards a partnership between training and line management to aid evaluation processes. For example, Frizzell go through an explicit process of 'contracting' between the training function and the line, where programmes are devised and prioritised against the business needs and strategy. Abernathy (1999) also quotes organisations saying 'any good manager knows how her work unit is performing and is paid to make some well-informed judgements about what's causing the performance to change'.

Dixon (1996) comments on another trend in organisations, which is towards certification of courses and the consequential need for more testing. She cites various companies who use tests extensively. Motorola have testing on one-third of their courses and aim to increase this to 100 per cent in the future. FPL Nuclear use tests to look at retention and ability. IBM use competency evidence as a way to certify project management skills. Dixon argues that best-practice companies are using level 3 and 4 evaluation selectively rather than consistently. Data collection needs to be customised and is therefore time-consuming and costly, requiring close collaboration with the clients. At Arthur Anderson, level 3 and 4 are measured less than ten per cent of the time, but the results have been very useful to them in increasing customer confidence generally.

Lee's study for the CIPD found that despite organisations talking about the need to measure the benefits of training in financial terms, in organisations with a degree of training maturity, the evidence is that managers are more interested in training to support business strategy. He argued that it may be counter-productive to have a narrow focus on financial outcomes whereby cultural benefits may be lost.

6.2 Conclusions for organisations

This review indicates that whilst a diversity of terminology and categories are used, there are huge areas of similarity in the range of evaluation models on offer, and evaluation strategies do not appear to have changed significantly in the last 40 years.

Having said that, there are some significant trends in the way organisations are approaching evaluation. Whilst the models used remain largely similar, there have been significant shifts towards laying the foundations for evaluation before the training programme takes place, and ensuring that training and development are more focused on the needs of the business. The emphasis in the literature on tying training needs to business requirements and making the objectives more explicit to allow ease of measurement, are examples of good practice which are now more frequently employed prior to any evaluation taking place. Whether or not these pre-stages should form part of an evaluation model, as in those of the Industrial Society, KPMT and CIRO models, or whether they form part of a wider HR and training needs analysis, is a question of debate. What is now evident is that evaluation needs to be considered carefully at the start of any process and well before the training and development solution is implemented. There is a difference between a model of the learning process that acknowledges that each stage is linked and influenced by the stages that precede it, and a model of evaluation that focuses on possible response measures at each of these different stages (see Figures 4.3 and 4.4). More recent evaluation models that extend the Kirkpatrick model back into the assessment of development need, are acknowledging the importance of this stage for the subsequent design and delivery of development interventions and their impact rather than suggesting that evaluation assesses them directly.

In terms of Kirkpatrick's four levels, the literature suggests that the model is still very useful in framing the different points at which measurement can take place. A question remains over the usefulness of measuring at the reaction level. Research here shows quite clearly that data can be misleading and responses may have little relationship with the future application of learning. Despite this, companies are still keen to get a sense of reactions to training and, used with caution, well-written reactionnaires can provide useful information on the extent to which the objectives were perceived to be met and why. The evidence from the literature is that organisations need to think quite carefully about what they want to measure, and to devise an instrument that picks up relevant criteria.

This review has also highlighted some of the intervening variables that have an impact on the effectiveness of training and learning transfer. Unless companies are seeking highly rigorous evaluations, it is not suggested that these are built into an evaluation model. However, factors such as self-efficacy, motivation, the transfer climate and learning goals, do need to be taken into account when considering the impact of any programme. The important message is that the more organisations can do to increase factors such as management support and participant involvement, the more likely it is that behavioural change will occur.

There are opposing views on the use of higher level and hard measures to evaluate the impact of training. Suggestions that models should include societal impact or focus primarily on return on investment, may well be appropriate in certain contexts. However, the evidence from organisations is that companies rarely undertake such evaluations and are being more selective about when to use such measures. Instead, they are moving more towards a responsive evaluation model, as suggested by Pulley, where the needs of the internal customer dictate the appropriateness of a particular approach. With transformational programmes in particular, the approach to evaluation needs to be carefully planned, and is unlikely to rely on hard data.

Whilst the different models of evaluation do provide more guidance on how to measure each level, there is little evidence of evaluation studies using pre- and post-testing with control groups in organisations, beyond a few more academic studies. It is more apparent that tools such as manager and self ratings, and 360 degree feedback, are growing in popularity as a means of measuring behavioural change. Worryingly, the literature cautions against the sensitivities of such measures, although the increased involvement of line managers in the design of the evaluation process may help to combat some of these difficulties.

In terms of the selection of a particular evaluation model or level of evaluation, the literature and practice suggest that the approach should depend on a number of different variables. Nickols (2000) sums the position up well. He states that there is 'no cookbook approach to evaluation of training … to properly evaluate requires one to think through the purposes of the training, the purposes of the evaluation, the audiences for the results of the evaluation, the points at which measurements will be taken, the time perspective to be employed and the overall framework to be utilised.' We would argue that, despite considerable criticism in the literature, the Kirkpatrick model remains useful for framing approaches to training and development evaluation. Consideration of the chain of impact, from articulation of development need, to impact on the organisation, can help focus the questions to ask and the means by which to answer them.

Evaluators should seek to conduct the most informative evaluation possible, given their differing needs and the constraints of the situation.

Bibliography

Abernathy D J (1999), 'Thinking outside the evaluation box', *Training and Development*, Vol. 53(2), February, pp. 18-23

Alliger G M, Janak E A (1989), 'Kirkpatrick's levels of training criteria: thirty years later', *Personnel Psychology*, Vol. 42 (2), pp. 331-342

Axtell C M, Maitlis S, Yearta S K (1997), 'Predicting immediate and longer-term transfer of training', *Personnel Review*, Vol. 26(3), pp. 201-213

Bassi L J, Cheney S (1997), 'Benchmarking the best', *Training and Development*, Vol. 51(11), pp. 60-64

Bee F, Bee R (1994), *Training Needs Analysis and Evaluation*, IPD

Bernthal P R (1995), 'Evaluation that goes the distance', *Training and Development*, Vol. 49(9), pp. 41-45

Blanchard P N, Thacker J W, Way S A (2000), 'Training evaluation: perspectives and evidence from Canada', *International Journal of Training and Development*, Vol. 4(4), pp. 295-304

Bourner T (1998), 'Bridges and Towers: Action Learning and Personal Development in HE', Inaugural Lecture, 24 November 1998

Brinkerhoff R, Dressler D (1990), *Productivity measurement: a guide for managers and evaluators*, Newbury Park, CA, Sage

Brinkerhoff R (1987), *Achieving Results From Training* San Francisco, Jossey-Bass

Bushnell D S (1990), 'Input, process, output: a model for evaluating training', *Training and Development Journal*, Vol. 44(3), March, pp. 41-43

Carless S A, Robert-Thompson G P (2001), 'Self ratings in training programs: an examination of level of performance and the effects of feedback', *International Journal of Selection and Assessment*, Vol. 9 (3), September

Clement R (1982), 'Testing the hierarchy theory of training evaluation: an expanded role for trainee reactions', *Public Personnel Management Journal*, Vol. 12 (2), pp. 176-184

Dawson R (1995), 'Fill this in before you go: under-utilized evaluation sheets', *Journal of European Industrial Training*, Vol. 19, No. 2

Deloitte, Haskins and Sells (1989), *Training in Britain: Employer Survey*, Training Agency, Sheffield

Dixon N M (1996), 'New routes to evaluation', *Training and Development*, Vol. 50(5), pp. 82-85

Department for Trade and Industry (2001), *UK Competitiveness Indicators*

Erikson P R (1990), 'Evaluating Training Results', *Training and Development Journal*, Vol. 44(1), pp. 57-59

Falkoner H (1997), 'Man with a plan', *Personnel Today*, 16 October

Falletta S V (1998), 'Evaluating training programs: the four levels by Kirkpatrick', *American Journal of Evaluation*, Vol. 19(2), pp. 259-261

Fitz-enz J (1994), 'Yes, you can weigh training's value', *Training*, Vol. 31(7), pp. 54-58

Ghodsian D, Bjork R A, Benjamin A S (1997), 'Evaluating training during training: obstacles and opportunities', in Quinones M A, Ehrenstein A (eds), *Training for a Rapidly Changing Workplace: Applications of Psychological Research*, American Psychological Association, Washington DC

Gist M, Bavetta A G, Stevens C K (1990), 'Transfer training method: its influence on skill generalisation, skill repetition and performance level', *Personnel Psychology*, Vol. 43, pp. 501-523

Haccoun R R, Hamtiaux T (1994), 'Optimizing knowledge tests for inferring learning acquisition levels in single group training evaluation designs: the internal referencing strategy', *Personnel Psychology*, Vol. 47, pp. 593-604

Hall B, LeCavalier J (2000), 'The Benchmarking Study of Best Practices: eLearning across the enterprise', *e-learning*, September

Hamblin A C (1974), *Evaluation and Control of Training*, McGraw Hill

Holton E F (1996), 'The flawed four-level evaluation model', *Human Resource Development Quarterly*, Vol. 7(1), pp. 5-21, Spring

Industrial Society (2000), *Managing Best Practice: Training Evaluation*, no. 70, April

Kaplan R S, Norton D (1996), *The Balanced Scorecard*, Harvard Business School Press

Kaufman R, Keller J M (1994), 'Levels of evaluation: beyond Kirkpatrick', *Human Resource Development Quarterly*, Vol. 5(4), Winter

Kaufman R, Keller J M, Watkins R (1995), 'What works and what doesn't: evaluation beyond Kirkpatrick', *Performance and Instruction*, Vol. 35(2), pp. 8-12

Kearns P, Miller T (1997), 'Measuring the impact of training and development on the bottom line', *FT Management Briefings*, Pitman Publishing, London

Kirkpatrick D L (1983), 'Four steps to measuring training effectiveness', *Personnel Administrator*, Vol. 28(11), pp. 19-25

Kirkpatrick D L (1996), 'Great ideas revisited: revisiting Kirkpatrick's four-level model', *Training and Development*, Vol. 50 (1), January, pp. 54-57

Kraiger K, Aguinis H (2001), 'Training effectiveness: Assessing training needs, motivation, and accomplishments', in London M (ed.), *How People Evaluate Others in Organizations*, pp. 203-220, Lawrence Erlbaum

Kraiger K, Ford J K, Salas E (1993), 'Application of cognitive, skill-based, and affective theories of learning outcomes to new methods of training evaluation', *Journal of Applied Psychology*, Vol. 78(2), pp. 311-328

Kraiger K, Jung K (1997), 'Linking training objectives to evaluation', in Quinones M A, Ehrenstein A (eds), *Training for a Rapidly Changing Workplace: Applications of Psychological*

Research, American Psychological Association, Washington DC

Lee R (1994), *Issues in People Management: What Makes Training Pay?*, Institute of Personnel and Development, No. 11

Lee S H, Pershing J A (1999), 'Effective reaction evaluation in evaluating training programmes: purposes and dimension classification', *Performance Improvement*, Vol. 38 (8), pp. 32-39

Lee S H, Pershing J A (2000), 'Evaluation of corporate training programs: perspectives and issues for further research', *Performance Improvement Quarterly*, 13(3), pp. 244-260

Levin H M (1983), *Cost-Effectiveness. A Primer*, Sage

Mabey C, Thomson A (2001), *The Learning Manager*, Institute of Management

Manpower Services Commission (1981^3), *Glossary of Training Terms*, HMSO, London

Marginson H, Armstrong H, Edwards R J, Purcell J, Hubbard C H (1993), *The Control of Industrial Relations in Large Companies: an Initial Analysis of the Second Company Level Industrial Relations Survey*, Warwick Paper No. 45 in Industrial Relations

Ministry of Defence (2001), *Training and Evaluation Toolkit*, July

Moad J (1995), 'Calculating the real benefit of training', *Datamation*, April 15

Molenda M, Pershing J, Reigeluth C (1996), 'Designing instructional systems', in Craig R (ed.), *The ASTD Training and Development Handbook: a Guide to Human Resource Development* (4th edn), New York, McGraw Hill

Morrow C C, Jarrett M Q, Rupinski M T (1997), 'An investigation of the effect and economic utility of corporate-wide training', *Personnel Psychology*, Vol. 50, pp. 91-119

Mumford A (1997), *How to Choose the Right Development Method*, Honey, Maidenhead

Newby A C (1992), *Training Evaluation Handbook*, Gower

Nickols F (2000), 'Evaluating training: there is no "cookbook" approach', http://home.att.net/~nickols/evaluate.htm

Noonan L E, Sulsky L M (2001), 'Impact of frame-of-reference and behavioural observation training on alternative training effectiveness criteria in a Canadian military sample', *Human Performance*, 14(1), pp. 3-26

Ostroff C (1991), 'Training effectiveness measures and scoring schemes: a comparison', *Personnel Psychology*, Vol. 44, pp. 353-375

Phillips J (1983), *Handbook of training evaluation and measurement methods*, Gulf Publishing Co., Houston

Phillips J (1994), *ROI: The Search for Best Practice*, American Society for Training and Development

Phillips J, Holton E (1995), *In Action: Measuring Return on Investment, Vol. 1*, American Society for Training and Development

Phillips J (1996), 'Measuring the results of training', in Craig R (ed.), *The ASTD Training and Development Handbook*, (4th edn), New York, McGraw Hill

Plant R A, Ryan R J (1994), 'Who is evaluating training?', *Journal of European Industrial Training*, Vol. 18(5), pp. 27-30

Pollard E, Hillage J (2001), *Exploring e-Learning*, IES Report 376

Preskill H, Torres R T (1999), *Evaluative Inquiry for Learning in Organizations*, Sage

Pulley M L (1994), 'Navigating the evaluation rapids', *Training and Development*, Vol. 48(9), September, pp. 19-24

Quinones M (ed.) (1997), *Training for a Rapidly Changing Workplace: Applications of Psychological Research*, American Psychological Association, Washington DC

Rae L (1999), 'A radical approach to evaluation', *Training Journal*, December, pp. 28-30

Roland B (1994), Training Needs Analysis and Evaluation, Institute of Personnel and Development, London.

Rough J (1994), 'Measuring training from a new science perspective', *Journal for Quality and Participation*, Vol. 17(6), pp. 12-16

Sackett P R, Mullen E J (1993), 'Beyond formal experimental design: towards an expanded view of the training evaluation process', *Personnel Psychology*, Vol. 46, pp. 613-627

Salas E, Cannon-Bowers J A (2001), 'The science of training: a decade of progress', *Annual Review of Psychology*, Vol. 52, pp. 471-499

Salmon G (2001), 'Far from remote', *People Management*, 27 September

Schrock S A, Coscarelli W C (1989²), *Criteria Referenced Test Development: Technical and Legal Guidelines for Corporate Training and Certification*

Sleezer C M, Cipicchio D, Pitonyak D (1992), 'Customizing and implementing training evaluation', *Performance Improvement Quarterly*, 5(4), pp. 55-75

Sloman M (2001), 'Forewarned is forearmed: e-learning', *People Management*, 5 April

Spilsbury M (1995), *Measuring the Effectiveness of Training*, IES Report 282

Spitzer D R (1999), 'Embracing evaluation', *Training*, Vol. 36(6), pp. 42-47

Stokking K M (1996), 'Levels of evaluation: Kirkpatrick, Kaufman, Keller, and beyond', *Human Resource Development Quarterly*, Vol. 7(2), pp. 179-183

Stufflebeam D L, Foley W J, Gephart W J, Guba, E G, Hammond R L, Merriman H O, Provus M M (1971), *Educational Evaluation and Decision Making*, Itasca, Peacock

Tamkin P, Barber L (1998), *Learning to Manage*, IES Report 345

Tamkin P, Hillage J (1997), *Individual Commitment to Learning: Motivation and Rewards*, DfEE Research Report RR11

Tamkin P, Hillage J, Willison R (2002), *Indicators of Management Capability: Developing a Framework*, Council for Excellence in Management and Leadership

Tracey J, Tannenbaum S, Kavanagh M (1995), 'Applying trained skills on the job: The importance of the work environment', *Journal of Applied Psychology*, 80(2), pp. 239-252

Twitchell S, Holton E F, Trott J W (2000), 'Technical training evaluation practices in the United States', *Performance Improvement Quarterly*, 13(3), pp. 84-109

Warr P B, Allan C, Birdi K (1999), 'Predicting three levels of training outcome', *Journal of Occupational and Organizational Psychology*, Vol. 72, pp. 351-375

Warr P B, Bird M, Rackham N (1970), *The Evaluation of Management Training*, Gower

Watkins R, Leigh D, Foshay R, Kaufman R (1998), 'Kirkpatrick plus: evaluation and continuous improvement with a community focus', *Educational Technology Research and Development*, Vol. 46 (4), pp. 90-96

Wexley K N, Baldwin T T (1986), 'Post-training strategies for facilitating positive transfer: an empirical exploration', *Academy of Management Journal*, Vol. 29, pp. 508-520